Christmas in Hell

by Arthur Gordon

Mursia
Cornelsen
ASCHEHOUG
Biblioteksförlaget
KALEIDOSCOPE

CHRISTMAS IN HELL (Fiction Factory 6)

This book is part of the series FICTION FACTORY. See list of already published titles page 46.
A sound cassette is available for each title.

Danish ISBN: 87-7565-367-7
Swedish ISBN: 91-542-1296-0
German ISBN: 3-464-06969-9
Norwegian ISBN: 82-03-13531-5
Italian ISBN: 88-425-8098-8

A Perfect Day

Inside my head the guns are always firing, the blood is always flowing, and the war never stops. I'm afraid to sleep because when I sleep I dream. My dreams always turn into nightmares. The Great War may have ended in 1918 for everyone else, but, for me, it is still going on. I think about the past all the time. I remember the way things used to be. I remember the world before it went mad. I keep thinking of one special day. It seems like a million years ago.

It was a perfect summer day in England. It was very hot and the sun was shining brightly. The sky was a deep blue, a special blue. The kind you only see during the very best summers. It was the 29th of June 1914, and it was my birthday. I was twenty-one years of age.

The butler walked towards me across the thick green grass. He was carrying a large silver tray with crystal glasses full of freshly-made lemonade. My family and I were sitting in the shade under a very old and very big oak tree. In the distance, I could hear people working in our fields. My two sisters were playing chess. They were beautiful, just like my mother. My mother was reading; she spent most of her time reading. My father had built the new library just for her. I watched my father. He was asleep underneath his blanket. Soon, I would be the head of our family because my father was dying. I would have to leave the army, and take over the running of our business affairs. But that was in the future. Now it was summer. We all loved our big country house. We called it our 'Little piece of Paradise'.

"Here is the lemonade you ordered, Sir," said the butler. "I've brought *The Times* with me as well, Sir."

"Thank you, Hope. Tell the cook to start making dinner. The boys will soon be in from the lake. They'll be as hungry as young lions. It must be the country air. All they do is sail and eat, sail and eat. I wish it would rain, then my father could see his sons again!"

Hope smiled his little servant's smile and went back to the house. My two younger brothers had built their boat during the winter. All winter our London house had been full of their noise. It was strange my father did not complain once.

Father made his money in Africa. It took him over fifteen years. When he returned to England he only wanted one thing. He wanted to marry a beautiful and intelligent girl. That girl was my mother. Father had a fantastic talent for making money, like some people have a talent for making good shoes.

"Mother, have you ever heard of a place called – Sarajevo?"

"No, my dear, I haven't. Is it important?"

"It's the name of a town in Bosnia, in the east of the Austrian Empire. Archduke Franz Ferdinand, the heir to the Austrian throne, was murdered there yesterday; his young wife was killed too. They were both shot in cold blood. *The Times* is full of the story."

"How terrible, what a tragedy. These socialists and anarchists love to kill. They throw their bombs, shoot people, and scream about 'Revolution', that's all they are good for. All they want to do is destroy. Their "Revolution" will be nothing but blood. It will be like the French Revolution – only a thousand times more horrible!"

My mother hated the socialists, anarchists and terrorists. She was afraid of them too. That was why she wanted me in the army.

Suddenly my father was awake, and talking very loudly.

"Revolution – has it come? Always said it would. Arthur, there are £ 5,000 in gold coins in the strong-box under my bed. You know where the guns are, my boy. Fight for the house and fight for your sisters. The swine will stop at nothing now!"

My father's face was red with anger and he was sweating hard. I jumped to my feet and ran over to him.

"Calm down, Father, please. Everything is all right. There is no need to worry about anything. There is no revolution. We were just talking about what happened in Bosnia..."

"What happened in Bosnia?!" he snapped.

"Nothing of any real importance. Franz Ferdinand was shot by terrorists. But don't you worry about it. Bosnia is a long, long, way from England. Look, Father, the sun is still shining here. Nothing has changed."

My father's face turned blue! He was now even more angry. He shouted at us with all his old strength, and tried to get out of his chair.

"Don't worry? Are you all fools? Don't talk to me like I'm a child. Damn it, my children are all idiots. They understand nothing. I might as well have stayed in Africa. This means war, boy! It's a spark, Arthur. Soon Europe will be burning from Paris to Moscow. Our world is coming to an end, Arthur. Remember my words, Arthur, remember my words…"

My mother was now beside my father. My two sisters were there too. I could hear my brothers running up from the lake. My father's lips were moving, but no sounds came from his mouth. My mother turned to me and said:

"Arthur, take your new automobile and go and get the doctor. I fear your father is dying!"

It was true. That night my father died. I never heard him say another word. Before he died he wrote me a note. There was only one word – 'Guns'. I knew instinctively what he wanted me to do. The next day I bought a machine-gun factory.

My father was right. War did come. The terrorists who killed the Archduke came from Serbia. Serbia was a little country next to Bosnia. How stupid it was. Two tiny countries started a world war! I wonder if anyone will remember Serbia and Bosnia in a hundred years?

The war broke out between Austria and Serbia. The Serbians asked the Russians to help them. The Austrians asked the Germans to help them fight the Russians. The Russians were allied with the French. We, the British, were allied with the French and the Russians. It was all very complicated and very absurd. I still don't understand precisely how it started. I never met anyone who did!

By August we were fighting Germans. The last words my mother said to me were,

"Don't worry, Arthur. You'll soon teach the Germans a lesson. You'll all be home before Christmas."

Then she kissed me and I sailed away to France.

In August the weather was wonderful in France. I liked France, the countryside is magnificent. But, like most Englishmen, I disliked the French. It's ironic that we were allied with people we didn't actually like very much!

In France

Many, many things have happened to me since August. I've seen many battles. I've seen many men get killed. They too thought they would be home for Christmas. Now they will never go home. Wars never go according to a plan. They never have, and they never will. It's so hard to believe that so many men have been killed. In August the French army wore blue jackets, bright red trousers, and white caps on their heads. The same uniforms they wore at Waterloo under Napoleon! They looked wonderful in their pretty uniforms. Like rows of toy soldiers on a table-top. They made wonderful targets too. The German machine-gunners could not miss them. It was just pure slaughter. Someone once told me that the German machine-gunners cried as they fired. I wonder if it was a true story? After over 100,000 Frenchmen had been killed, they changed their uniforms. Now they wear a dirty blue/grey. The days of pretty uniforms are gone forever. There are no pretty colours anymore on this battlefield.

My mother was wrong. It's Christmas, and I'm not at home. I'm sitting in a stinking hole in the ground. There are millions of holes in Europe and millions of men are sitting in them. The battlefield stretches from Switzerland to the North Sea. It is an enormous open wound across the face of Europe. The scar will last forever, and nothing will ever be the same again. Europe is a continent committing suicide!

Ra-ta-ta-ta, ra-ta-ta-ta, ra-ta-ta-ta.

I knew the sound. It was a German machine-gun. It was the sound of death. The sound of the devil laughing at us.

Ra-ta-ta-ta, ra-ta-ta-ta, ra-ta-ta-ta.

"Excuse me, Sir. There is a message from Head Quarters, Sir. I've brought you a nice cup of tea as well, Sir."

I looked up into Sergeant Tompkins' face. He was smiling at me. Tompkins always smiled. He was always telling jokes. I don't see anything funny in this war. I get depressed. I think too much. A soldier should not think too much. Too much thinking is bad for you. It can stop you killing, and killing is a soldier's job. I wish I was like Tompkins. He is a fighting machine. He hates all Germans. He likes killing them. I've heard him say a thousand times, "The only good German is a dead one!" I think he actually be-

lieves it. One day I will tell him that our King's family are German. Their family name is Battenburg. The German Kaiser is the King's cousin! This war is really a family fight between the Battenburgs. How did everybody else get involved? The whole thing would be funny – if it wasn't so tragic!

I read the message. I smiled to myself.

"Good news, Sir?"

"Yes, Sergeant. It is good news. We are going to have a little holiday. We are going to stop fighting because it is Christmas. We are all Christians, and at Christmas Christians don't kill, Sergeant."

I looked into Tompkins' face. He almost looked sad. He looked surprised. Then he said.

"Why have we got to stop fighting, Sir?"

There were times when I hated Tompkins more than the Germans!

"It's Christmas, Tompkins. You remember *Christmas*, don't you? It's the time of peace and goodwill to all men. No one gets killed at Christmas, it wouldn't be right, would it? After all, we are all God's children, aren't we, Sergeant?"

"Do you mean the Germans as well, Sir?"

Now I did not understand.

"What about the Germans, Sergeant?"

"Are the Germans God's children too, Sir?

Just like us? I mean, Sir – they are Huns. They murdered babies when they invaded Belgium. They slaughtered unarmed civilians: men, women and children. We read all about it in the newspapers. The Germans aren't civilised, Sir. They aren't like us. They're barbarians. They're not *real* Christians, Sir. They can't be, Sir, can they?"

My God, I thought to myself. Tompkins actually believed our propaganda! He believed it! He believed that the Germans marched through Belgium with babies stuck onto their bayonets! Now I had the proof: Being a soldier and having a brain did not go together!

"Do you always believe what you read in the newspapers, Sergeant?"

"Yes, Sir, they wouldn't print it if it wasn't true, would they, Sir?"

I wanted to say something, but I was too tired. It was too late to talk now. We should have talked before the war. Now talking was useless. The gunfire had drowned the sound of our voices.

Men of Steel

The evil machine-gun started to fire again.

Ra-ta-ta-ta, ra-ta-ta-ta, ra-ta-ta-ta.

"Go and tell the men the good news, Sergeant. Tell them to be very careful. Tell them to keep their heads down. The cease-fire begins in two hours. I don't want anyone to be killed at Christmas!"

"Yes, Sir, very good, Sir. I'll pass the word along to the men, Sir."

Tompkins saluted and marched away. I was glad to see him go. I didn't really like him. I was sure he didn't like me. I was too soft to be a real soldier. Tompkins was a real soldier. He was made of steel all the way through.

I drank some of my tea. It was hot and very sweet. Tompkins always put too much sugar in my tea. He gave me his ration. When this war is over, I will send him a wagon full of sugar. I will dump it in his front garden!

I laughed to myself. I try not to laugh out loud. Officers should not laugh out loud. The men might think we were going mad. We *are* all going mad, but it's best that the men don't find out!

The men laugh a lot. Their humour is black. They make jokes about everything, though mostly about sex and death. The first there is too little of, the second there is too much of. Maybe laughter helps to keep them going. I once asked one of them why they made jokes.

"Is war and the battlefield so funny?"

He stopped smiling at once. Suddenly he became very serious. His face changed. His voice became different. Even the expression in his eyes was different.

"No, Sir, the war isn't funny. It's horrible, Sir. It's stupid as well. We all know that, Sir. But we can't do anything about it can we, Sir? We can't just go home, can we, Sir? You have to laugh, don't you, Sir? You have to laugh or you would cry, and crying is no use, is it, Sir?"

I think that is why the lower classes have so much humour. Crying *is* useless. Make the best of life. Try to see the funny side of everything. Laughter makes their lives worth living. It helps them to survive. Laughter is like opium for them. I wish I found laughter so easy.

I was not brought up to laugh at my life. I was trained to take my life seriously. I was trained to control my life. I'm rich and powerful. But now, here in this terrible place, I'm just like the men, a tiny part of an enormous killing machine. A machine which I cannot control. I wish I could laugh like the men, but I can't.

My opium comes in a little silver bottle which I keep in my pocket. One, two, three crystal-clear drops in my tea-cup. They float on the surface for a moment, then, like three little fishes, they dive to the depths of my cup. In a way they are like us, here for a moment, then gone, who knows where.

Ra-ta-ta-ta, ra-ta-ta-ta, ra-ta-ta-ta.

That bloody machine-gun again. I wish I'd never bought the machine-gun factory. When the war is over, I'll sell it to someone else.

Flying Away

It is Christmas Eve and it is very cold. There are no clouds. The sky is very beautiful. I wish I had a telescope with me. Looking at the sky is better than looking at the battlefield. I can see my dreams in the sky. In my dreams, there is no blood and no mud. I'd like to go to sleep for a long time. Then one day I would wake up. I would ask people about the war, "Who won?" They would look at me as if I were mad. "What war? We don't have wars anymore. The last 'war' was a thousand years ago. No one remembers who won. Is it important?"

I can see the Milky Way. I wish I could fly up to the stars. I would run along this trench. I would run as fast as I could. Faster and faster I would run. Then at last I would jump into the air. Like a bird I would fly away. I would leave this hole in the ground, leave this ugly battlefield. I would leave France below me. Higher and higher I would fly. I would then look down on Europe and laugh. I would fly far away from the world. Up, up I would go, up to the Milky Way. I would go past the stars. Then on and on and on…

In Tibet, there are monks who can fly. They can fly because they *want* to fly. They concentrate for years. They think of nothing else but flying. One day, when they are ready, they go outside, and they *fly*. I will go to Tibet when this stupid war is over and I will learn to fly!

Then I heard an angel singing! It had a very beautiful voice. It was high and clear. It was singing in a strange language, a language I did not understand. I always thought that angels sang in English. I mean God speaks English, so why don't angels sing in English?

Then I realised, I understood. The angel was singing in German! Then I heard another voice. Someone was speaking to me. I opened my eyes. Sergeant Tompkins was standing beside me. He said,

"He's got a good voice, hasn't he, Sir? I mean for a German."

It wasn't an angel that was singing, it was a German soldier. I had been dreaming again. I seem to dream all the time now. I think it must be the opium. I was wounded in the head at the beginning of the war. I still have three little pieces of metal behind my right ear. I sometimes get terrible headaches. I feel like my head is a-bout to explode. My little silver bottle with its magic drops stops me from going mad.

"Do you recognise the song, Sergeant?" I asked.

"Yes, Sir, it's "Silent Night". A beautiful English Christmas carol"

"I think the Germans call it 'Stille Nacht', Sergeant. They think it's a German song."

"Do they, Sir? Well that shows that the Huns know nothing about music. They know nothing about real fighting either. They are afraid of cold steel. They run like rabbits whenever they see an English bayonet. I remember, it was last week, I took my bayonet and..."

"Thank you, Sergeant, I don't want to hear the unpleasant details. You can go now."

Tompkins marched away. I was glad to see the back of him. He was the perfect soldier for the perfect war.

The German soldier stopped singing. I turned and looked up at the stars again. I heard another fine voice. This time it was an English soldier. He was singing 'Stille Nacht' in English. His voice was good too. The voice could be heard all over the battlefield. Sounds travel far at night. Big, clean snowflakes started to fall from heaven. Soon the whole battlefield was pure again. All the dirt was covered up. For the first time it felt like Christmas.

The English soldier stopped singing. His song was over. Everything was silent again. I felt cold and rubbed my hands together. Suddenly someone was shouting. It was a German, I could tell from his accent. He was shouting in English. The German lines were only fifty metres away.

"Hello, Tommy" he shouted. None of our men answered. He tried again.

"Hello, Tommy, Happy Christmas!"

This time one of our men answered.

"Happy Christmas, Fritz. What's the weather like over there?"

"Cold, Tommy. My toes are like ice. The Kaiser has promised me a pair of woollen socks. He is making them for me himself. The Kaiser takes good care of his men!"

He was making a joke. We always thought the Germans had no sense of humour. I heard lots of laughter from the German side. My men started to laugh too. Soon everyone was laughing, all around me there was laughter. So the Germans laugh *too*. I had almost forgotten they were human, just like us.

The laughter stopped. I held out my hand. A big, white snowflake landed silently on my palm.

I watched it silently melting. My mother told me they were angel's tears. I looked over at the German lines. The moon was big and bright. There was a lot of light. It was almost like daytime. I could see very clearly. I saw a man climb out of the German trenches! He had his hands in the air. He did not have a rifle. He started to walk over to us. He was obviously mad, or a deserter!

Something hit the ground in front of me. I rubbed my eyes and I looked again. It was hard to believe. It was not a bomb or a grenade. It was a long, thick, German sausage!

"Enjoy the sausage, Tommy," a German shouted over.

"What's it taste like, Fritz?" one of our men asked.

"Have you never had German sausage, Tommy?"

"I've never had anything German, Fritz, except your bloody bullets!"

All the men on our side started to laugh again. So did the Germans. Everyone was having a good time. Christmas was a magic, special time for all.

"No Man's Land"

Time went by. I looked into 'No Man's Land' again. It was full of German soldiers! None of them were carrying weapons. They just stood and looked over at us. They were waiting for something. I looked at the machine-gun. All I had to do was press the trigger. I could kill hundreds of them. I would be a hero. I would get a medal. I looked at my watch. It was 22.30; the cease-fire had begun. To open fire now would be murder. I would be a criminal, *not* a hero. I was five minutes too late. It was funny. Five minutes separated the 'Hero' from the 'Criminal'.

I stood up too. I climbed up out of my hole in the ground. Now I too was standing in 'No Man's Land,' and no one was shooting at me. It felt very strange. The whole scene was unreal. Where had all the bullets gone? I walked towards the German sausage. I bent down and picked it up. I held it close to my nose. It smelled good. I had not eaten German sausage for years. The last time was in Dresden. It seems a lifetime ago.

Hundreds of English eyes were looking at me. I started to walk over to the Germans. I looked behind me. Slowly, my men were following me out into 'No Man's Land'. They had left their weapons behind too. There was no pistol in my hand. There was only a German sausage! At last I reached the Germans. I stopped and looked at them. They stood and looked at me. I felt like an animal in the zoo!

"Haven't you ever seen an Englishman before?" I asked.

A German said,

"Not as close as this. Not for a long time. I'm used to seeing dead Englishmen!"

Then a very tall and very handsome officer stepped forward. He smiled and held out his hand. We shook hands. His hand felt strong and warm. Now I knew I was awake. I was not daydreaming. It was all really happening!

"My name is Otto von Mayerling. I'm so pleased to meet you. The weather is a bit cold, isn't it?"

His English was almost perfect, except for a slight accent.

"English people don't *always* talk about the weather," I answered.

"Oh, I'm sorry. I couldn't think of anything else to say. I just said the first thing that came into my head. I'm a bit nervous you see. This is an unusual situation. I mean, you are the enemy. A few minutes ago I would have shot you, now we are standing and talking like we are in Oxford Street. It is all very strange, don't you think?"

"Christmas is a special time," I said. "We are celebrating the birth of Jesus, he was going to save mankind, he died to save us. Now we are destroying ourselves."

"But *not* at Christmas. Now we remember that we are human and not just killing machines."

We both smiled at each other. Otto von Mayerling was about my age. He was taller than I was. He looked like my brother George. The same boyish good looks. George had been killed in September.

"We shouldn't be doing this. Fraternising with the enemy is wrong. Who knows where it might lead us," he said.

"I know it's wrong. That's why I like it. Listen, I won't tell the Kaiser, if you promise not to tell my King!"

"All right, I agree. We will both forget about the war. We may not be here next year."

"I know, we may all be dead, and no one will

remember, or care about what we did, or why we did it."

"No I didn't mean that," said Otto. "I mean the war will be over by next Christmas. It can't last another year, can it?"

"This war will go on forever. We are destroying Europe. This is the century of destruction."

"You *are* depressed," said Otto. "Here, take some of this."

He gave me a bottle of snaps which he had inside the pocket of his long coat.

"My family make it. It's the best in all Germany," he said with great pride.

"That's strange," I said. "We own a whisky factory in Scotland. Where do you come from in Germany?"

"Our factory is in Dresden. Dresden is a beautiful city. I'm glad it's a long way away. The guns cannot reach it. Dresden will never be destroyed."

"If this war lasts long enough, Dresden will be destroyed."

"Look," said Otto, "Forget the war. Next Christmas when it is over, come to Dresden. Come and see our new factory. It's very modern. You will find it very interesting. We will become great friends."

" All right," I replied. I tried to sound optimis-

tic. "I will come to Dresden. Now all you have to do is talk to the Kaiser and get him to stop the war."

"And you must tell the King that we all want to go home. This is no place to spend Christmas!"

We both laughed, and drank more snaps from Otto's bottle.

After a few seconds, Otto suddenly smiled and said,

"I've just had an idea. Let's meet here tomorrow and have a good game of football. What do you think?"

I smiled at his absurd idea and nodded.

"You won't win the war," I said. "And you won't win the match tomorrow. We British invented football!"

"You British think you invented *everything*. Wait until tomorrow, we'll teach you a lesson you will never forget. Just wait and see, my friend!"

We drank more of the snaps. We ate sausage. We drank more snaps. We talked a lot. We talked about Dresden and about London. I forgot how cold it was. I forgot where we were. We kept on drinking. The bottle slowly emptied. I got drunk. Otto got drunk. To find a friend in hell is good, it's almost like being in heaven!

All around us the men were enjoying themselves. They were talking. They were drinking. They were eating. Germans were eating English pork pies. Englishmen were eating German sausages. I liked the world again. I liked myself again. The moon grew bigger and bigger. The stars got brighter and brighter. There was so much light. The two angels started to sing again, in English *and* in German. And I went into the clear, white light.

A Day to Remember

Slowly, very slowly I opened my eyes. The clear, white light was gone. I knew where I was. I was in my bed. How did I get there? I didn't remember. Somebody must have carried me there. I was safe in my bunker. I dragged myself out of my bed. My corporal came into my underground room.

"Good morning, Sir. Breakfast is almost ready. I managed to find you an egg, Sir. There's hot water for you to wash and shave in, and I've got your best uniform ready, Sir. I've polished your boots too, Sir. I want you to look nice for Christmas, Sir."

"Corporal Slicker," I said. "You will make someone a wonderful wife!"

"Yes, Sir, thank you, Sir. I try to do my best, and I can tell you, Sir, it isn't easy. The conditions here are terrible, Sir. Yesterday I had a horrible experience. I..."

"Thank you, Corporal Slicker, that will be all for now. I'll call you if I need anything. You can go."

Slicker was an irritating little man, but he

made a good breakfast. Before he joined the army he had been a butler. He was still a wonderful servant. He did everything to please me. Normally I patted him on the head like a dog. I would say a few kind words, but today was different. I had a hangover. My head was splitting down the middle. I reached for my little silver bottle. One, two, three, four, five tiny drops in my tea. I ate my breakfast slowly. I wasn't very hungry. The hot tea was what I really needed. Tea is so refreshing. I drank three cups. I was soon feeling alive again, and my headache was gone too. Now I could face the world above me with a smile.

Slowly I climbed the ladder to the upper world. My bunker was thirty feet below the ground. I finally reached the surface. I let my eyes get used to the light. I looked around me. Everything was the same, what a shame! Sergeant Tompkins marched towards me. Soon he would start to speak. I felt for my little silver friend. My fingers found it in my pocket. I felt better at once.

"Good morning, Sir. Lovely morning, Sir. No problems, Sir. Everything quiet, Sir."

"Why should there be any problems, Sergeant? It's Christmas, remember? Christmas is a time of peace, not war. There is a cease-fire."

"I know, Sir, but I don't trust the Huns. They are liars and cheats the lot of them. Their word don't mean a thing. Look what they did to Belgium, Sir. Belgium was neutral too. What I say is, the only good German is a..."

"I *know,* Sergeant. I *know* what you say. I know what you mean. I've heard it all a thousand times before. Look here, man, why don't you go and do something useful – go and polish your bayonet. Then when it's nice and clean and sharp, take your bayonet and..."

"May I ask a question, Sir?"

"Yes, what is it now?"

"The men think there is going to be a football match. I told them not to be so stupid, but they keep talking about it. It's football, football and more football. If you told the men, Sir, I'm sure they would stop all this nonsense. You see the men don't understand, Sir."

"Understand what, Sergeant?"

"We are fighting a war, Sir. We are here to kill Germans. The more we kill the quicker we will win the war. Then we can all go home. We didn't come here to play football with them. I say that the idea is dangerous nonsense, Sir!"

"It's *my* idea, Sergeant," I said.

Tompkins' face changed. Now *he* did not understand. He was intensely angry. I swear I saw steam coming out of his ears! I had never seen anybody so angry in my life. Not even my father!

"Look, Tompkins, the men need to relax. They need to have some fun. They need something to look forward to, something positive. They cannot think of war all the time. It will all be over tomorrow. Tomorrow we can go back to killing each other, like good soldiers should."

"But, Sir ..."

"Look, Sergeant, There are no 'buts'. I am in charge here. I'm the officer. I give the orders. You do as I say. Is that clear, do you understand, Sergeant?"

"Yes, Sir, I understand, Sir. You want to do something good for the men. But what happens afterwards, Sir?"

"After what, Sergeant?"

"What will happen when Christmas is over? The cease-fire will be over tomorrow. Tomorrow the war will start again. Think about it, Sir. I beg you. Think about the men. Think of their feelings. Today we play football. Today we make friends. But tomorrow, tomorrow we have to start killing again. Tomorrow the men will have to kill the friends they make today. That is a terrible thing to do. It isn't good for morale, Sir."

"You mean it's easy to kill the "enemy", but hard to kill your friends?"

"Yes, Sir. That is precisely what I mean. I wouldn't shoot my neighbours."

"You're right, Sergeant. It's wrong to shoot your neighbours."

"Thank you, Sir. I'll go and tell the men the match is off."

"No, Sergeant Tompkins you won't. The men will have their football. I will give them *one* good, human day. A day they can remember forever."

"The generals in the High Command won't like it, Sir."

"The generals aren't in the front line – we are."

Tompkins marched off. I never wanted to see his face again.

Friendly Football

I sat thinking for a long time. I used not to think. I just enjoyed my life. Now I think all the time. I think too much. This war has made me think. Every minute may be your last. I feel old. I don't think I will ever be young again. The war has done that to millions of us. The ordinary soldiers are starting to think too. They are starting to ask questions. They are starting to question everything. Who will they blame for the war? Maybe they will blame me and my class? Maybe my father was right, perhaps this is the end of our world. Is it the start of a new one? Like a phoenix rising from the ashes?

I looked down at my watch. It was twelve o'clock. It was time for the match. I've never played football. At my school, we only played rugby. Football is a game for the masses. It is not a game for English gentlemen.

I began to walk towards the middle of 'No Man's Land'. I looked to my left. I looked to my right. There were soldiers everywhere. I saw Otto von Mayerling. He was practising with a ball. So he plays football, how strange.

"Hello, I said. "Isn't it a beautiful day?"

Otto looked at me and smiled and I thought of George.

"Yes, it is a wonderful day. Christmas Day and the sun is shining, we are very lucky. Today is a special day. We won't see a day like this for a long, long, long time."

It was a good game. The men were happy for a while. They kicked their ball around for hours. The goal posts were made of piles of coats and helmets. German and English all mixed together. I think there were about fifty players on each side.

It was all very undisciplined and chaotic. It's strange but I don't remember who won. Was it the Germans or was it us? I think we got about twenty-seven goals and the Germans about twenty-four. It might have been the other way around! As I said, football isn't my kind of game. I don't think the score really matters. Nobody remembers our game – why should they?

I looked at my watch. It was now four o'clock. In two hours the cease-fire would be over. There would be no more football. 'No Man's Land' would be for the dead, not the living. The match ended and Otto von Mayerling and I met once more.

"See, Arthur. I said I was a good player. I scored eleven goals. I don't do that everyday."

"Yes, Otto, but you won't win the war!" I replied.

Otto gave me his address in Dresden. I gave Otto my address in London. We talked very quickly and made lots of plans. We talked faster and faster. We wanted to say everything before it was too late. We had so many things to say and so little time. It's strange when you really need time it passes so quickly.

"The war will soon be over. We'll meet in London and go to an expensive restaurant and get very, very drunk. And I will carry you home again, my friend."

"Yes, you're right." I said. "The war will soon be over."

I think we both knew we were lying. Friends often lie to each other. Too much truth can be painful. Anyway, it was not the time for *truth*, we both wanted our dream to go on for as long as possible. We fought to keep reality out just a little bit longer.

I took my gold cigarette-case out of my pocket. It was very beautiful. I had been given it on my last birthday. It was a present from my brother George. My name was on the front – Arthur Britton. I handed the gold cigarette-case to Otto. He took a cigarette out and started to smoke.

"Keep the case," I said. "Think of it as a Christmas present. I hope you like it?"

Otto moved his fingers slowly and carefully over the fine gold case. Then he looked up at me and said,

"Thank you very, very much, Arthur. I will always keep it on me. Every time I smoke a cigarette I will think of you."

Then Otto put his hand inside his jacket. He pulled out a gold watch on a long, thick gold chain. He handed it over to me.

"This is my present for you, Arthur. It is a very fine old watch. It was my father's watch. Please take it. I want you to have it."

"Thank you, I like to know what the time is."

We shook hands and said 'goodbye'. Then we started to walk back to our own sides. I reached my hole in the ground. I turned around. I was all alone again. Then I saw a man. It was Otto. I could not see his face but I knew it was him. He waved to me. And he shouted,

"Merry Christmas and a Happy New Year!"

Then he climbed down into his hole in the ground and I did the same. My friend was gone and so was peace.

A Home for Heroes

All this happened a long time ago. It was ten years ago, to be precise. Sometimes I wonder if it ever really happened. Christmas 1914 was very strange. It was unique. It never happened again. Tompkins was right of course. The generals did not like what happened. It was not good for morale, fraternising with the enemy! The whole episode was kept quiet. The story did not appear in the newspapers. The journalists were under censorship. It was a dangerous secret. No one at home knew what happened until months afterwards. My men and I were moved back from the front line and we were ordered not to talk. Our little Christmas miracle was buried in silence.

The war lasted four more years. What followed was a slaughter never before seen on earth. Millions and millions of young men were killed and wounded. Sergeant Tompkins was killed. Corporal Slicker was killed. I lost two brothers to the war machine. But I survived. Many people tell me I was lucky. I am not so sure.

In 1918 the mighty German army started to collapse. The soldiers could give no more blood. They wanted to stop fighting and go home. Nobody remembered or cared about what they were fighting for. The soldiers were deserting in thousands. They went on strike too and began to talk of revolution. Otto joined the strike. He became an active revolutionary. Four long years of war had changed him, like they changed me and millions of others. Otto was put on trial and found guilty of treason. He was shot on a cold rainy morning. The last thing he wanted was a cigarette from his gold case. Nobody knows what happened to his body.

In Germany, the last weeks of the war were total chaos. The revolution was growing. The German generals and politicians were afraid. They were afraid that the Russian Revolution would spread to Germany. If that happened all Europe would fall to the revolutionaries. For a time I thought my father had been right. I really thought the end of my world had come. I was not sad. I was glad. The old one did not deserve to go on. But it did not happen. The revolution in Germany was brutally crushed. Slowly things returned to normal. The old world survived, but it was now a cripple. Eventually I went home. Home to a country fit for 'heroes' to live in.

Back to mass unemployment for the poor and the worst economic crisis in history.

Now I sit under the big, old oak tree in our garden. It's cold and I think autumn is coming. The lake is empty, my two brothers are gone. My mother just sits and reads all day, day after day after day. I never go to London now. I spend all my time in the country, in our 'Little piece of Paradise'. The war killed something inside me. One, two, three, four, five, six, seven little drops in my tea, from my little silver bottle. Here in the country, I have my memories for company. I live in the past because I hate the present and I fear the future. It's precisely one o'clock, and, yes this *is* a very fine gold watch.

FICTION FACTORY
– for today's and tomorrow's readers

We hope you enjoyed reading the book you have just finished.

Do you want to read more fascinating stories in an English which is just as easy to understand as your own language?

Here is a list of the first 16 books in the FICTION FACTORY series. The short descriptions can help you make your choice.

NIGHT ATTACK (Fiction Factory 1)

Michael Windsor

Will what first appears to be nothing more than a childish prank develop into something more serious?

Indian immigrant family Khan's dream of owning their very own little shop turns into a nightmare, when racism appears in the dark streets of London.

The Khan family wish only to live in peace, they do not want to have to fight. But when they find themselves standing with their backs to the wall they realize that action has to be taken and that they have to seek help whereever it is to be found.

THE COMPUTER KINGS (Fiction Factory 2)

Michael Windsor

Krishna Goldstar has only one aim in life: to win Venus Games' giant competition to find the world's very best computer-game players. Krishna wants to become one of the 'Computer Kings'.

But what starts as a game ends in terror, in a reality more horrifying than any computer-game. What is the terrible secret that lurks behind Venus Games and can it really be a threat to the whole world?

DRAGON ROCK (Fiction Factory 3)

Angela Wright

Judy Marshall is a promising young biologist at the famous university of Oxford. Her future is assured – far too assured for Judy's liking. She desires action and excitement in her life – just once, then she can return to her dusty desk again.

Judy's wish comes true. Soon she finds herself flying north towards the dark castle, Dragon Rock, on a top-secret mission for the government and to a meeting with a mad scientist!

THE RED FOX (Fiction Factory 4)

Jane Scott

The young Danish girl Pernille Karlsberg suddenly finds herself in another world when she moves to England to be reunited with her father.

The rural idyl of life in Honeybell Cottage is too good to last, and soon the realities of life in England force themselves onto Pernille.

Her new school and her friendship with a Lord put Pernille's principles and loyalty to the test.

SLAUGHTER IN SOWETO (Fiction Factory 5)

Michael Windsor

The revolution in South Africa as experienced by two young, black brothers, Marcus and John Ndanga. In this dramatic story we also meet their mother, a local priest, and a militant black activist. All of these characters create an exciting portrait of the conflicts that exist inside the black population, between generations, different political groups, and even in individual families.

A gigantic mass-funeral is attacked by the military, and soon a day of mourning is turned into a massacre and the two brothers are forced to run for their lives.

CHRISTMAS IN HELL (Fiction Factory 6)

Arthur Gordon

Christmas 1914. The First World War has broken out. Two enormous armies face each other separated by only a few feet of frozen mud. The place is a British trench where a young officer thinks about the hell he has been sucked into.

A Christmas cease-fire is agreed upon, and soon soldiers from both armies are openly fraternizing with each other. They meet in 'No-Man's-Land' and exchange gifts and jokes. Sworn ennemies become friends.

They agree to play football the following day – Christmas Day. It will be a 'friendly' match. However, not everyone on the British side is happy about such a 'dangerous' development.

TRAPPED! (Fiction Factory 7)

Sally Drewe

Jimmy Jenkins lives alone with his mother at the top of a block of flats which is rapidly turning into a slum. Jimmy's unemployed mother spends most of her time watching the television with only the small red pills that the doctor has given her for her 'nerves' for company.

Jimmy and his friends have to create their own 'entertainment' in this drab concrete environment. The boys terrorize the drunken old tramps who sit and drink in the garden of a dilapidated old house. Afterwards the boys play hide and seek, but Jimmy's hiding place is suddenly changed into a trap. He discovers that he cannot get out despite all his frantic efforts.

Will anyone hear Jimmy's scream for help? Will anyone come to Jimmy's aid? or will he remain – trapped?!

THE FLAMING CROSS (Fiction Factory 8)

Linda Blake

Beautiful young doctor Jane Jones leaves her comfortable existence in New York, in order to journey south, to the little isolated rural town of Hicksville. A place where she believes that she can do some good by treating the poor and giving advice to them.

Hicksville, indeed, is not New York. Many of the people have never seen a doctor. Jane really meets the challenge she wants in her life. She is soon in deadly conflict with the might of the Ku Klux Klan, who sentences her to death for her 'crimes.'

Now Jane really needs help. But who does one turn to in

a strange town? And who will dare help a 'baby killer' against the men of the Klan?

THE X-RAYS (Fiction Factory 9)

Jeff Starre

To succeed in the ultra-competitive world of rock-music is never easy, it's even more difficult when you're a girl. But Liz Black is very determined, very strong, and very talented.

Despite hard opposition Liz fights her way to the top gaining her place amongst the other superstars. But Liz pays a high price for her fame and fortune. Friendship and romance have to take second place, and she discovers how they can change into hatred and insanity.

We follow Liz from her schooldays, through the blackest nightmare, and up to the light at the biggest rock-festival of all time.

THE JUDGE'S DAUGHTER (Fiction Factory 10)

Peter Bullet

Private detective 'Dick' Pride is one day contacted by rich and powerful Judge Peter Buck. Judge Buck's beautiful young daughter Joy has run away from home. She has to be found regardless of the cost and without any scandal, as Judge Buck is a candidate for president.

Time runs fast. Life for a beautiful girl like Joy Buck in the teeming underworld of Los Angeles can be very dangerous and extremely short!

And what possible reason could she have for running away from her comfortable life and a loving father?

THE DEATH OF KING COAL (Fiction Factory 11)

John J. Graves

The Death of King Coal describes life in a small mining village in the North of England during the longest and most violent industrial dispute in this century, the 1984 miners' strike.

Teenagers Peter and Mary find themselves on opposite sides of an invisible line that divides the village in two. Peter's father is a striking miner, Mary's father is a policeman. They represent chief opponents in a bitter struggle over the future of the mine, the shutting of which will mean the death of the village.

Peter and Mary's personal relationship, attitudes and loyalties are put under strain in this dramatic story.

THE FALKLANDS WAR (Fiction Factory 12)

Arthur Gordon

Mick Jones joins the army in order to escape from Liverpool's sky-high unemployment. He is accepted by the elite parachute regiment, the famous 'Red Devils'. For the first time in his life Mick feels proud and respected.

Suddenly Mick and his friends find themselves sailing for the other side of the world to fight a war over a place they have never even heard of – the Falklands! A real war with Argentina, something that Mick never had dreamed would happen.

Micks attitude to the war changes radically as he is confronted with the tragedy of its violence and the sadistic Sergeant Seyton. One dark, rainswept night on the side of a grim mountain Mick is forced to choose between obeying orders and his conscience.

KING IN A CAGE (Fiction Factory 13)

John J. Graves

By the 1870's almost all of Southern Africa has been conquered by the British. Only one small area remains free, a wild mountainous desert. It is defended by what is left of the great Zulu army.

When gold is discovered there, Joseph Sharpton, the richest man in Africa, stops at nothing to get his hands on the land. At the same time he also decides that young Edwina Sweet shall become his wife. The idea makes her sick. But how can she resist a man with so much wealth and power? Can Edwina escape from him, or will she, like the rest of Southern Africa, come under his dominance?

CRAGSCAR (Fiction Factory 14)

Jane Scott

Margaret Marlowe was tired of her life. She was also tired of making atomic bombs. A nice, quiet holiday in a fishing village by the sea was what she needed.

However, Margaret soon discovers that she cannot escape her life just by running away. A mysterious illness among the local people draws Margaret into a dangerous intrigue involving the enormous Cragscar nuclear plant. Suddenly Margaret finds herself fighting against a 'monster' that she is also a part of!

COPS AND ROBBERS (Fiction Factory 15)

Peter Bullet

Another bank robbery has taken place in London. This time two guards have been shot. Dan Watts is an alcoholic crime reporter for one of the biggest newspapers in Britain. Dan is ordered to find the gang by the editor of his paper.

One black night he receives a mysterious telephone call. It is from a woman he has not seen for over ten years. She desperately needs his help and says she knows the identity of the robbers. Her amazing story leads Dan into danger and at the same time turns his whole world upside down!

WITCHFINDER (Fiction Factory 16)

Angela Wright

When antique dealer Andrea Elsen is given a wonderful and very beautiful old chair by Charlie Harder, she cannot imagine that it will drag her into terror. Into a world of witches and demons and danger!

Andrea finds herself fighting strange dreams which threaten to take over her life. The chair takes her back in time to face the horrors of the witch-hunt and the terrible Witchfinder General! Can Andrea escape, or will she burn like all the other witches?

WOMEN AT WAR (Fiction Factory 17)

Sally Drewe

A dramatic story from the militant suffragettes' fight for equal rights for women. An often bitter struggle with the authorities as experienced by a young British aristocrat, Lady Constance Welles. A young woman who because of her ideals is forced to change her whole way of thinking and lifestyle.

Lady Constance must leave home, family and title behind her when she decides to follow her 'sisters' in their battle for social justice.

THE CRYSTAL SHIP (Fiction Factory 18)

Jeff Starre

By the end of the twenty-first century industrial pollution and climatic changes have almost destroyed the planet Earth. A small group of young people hijack a starship in order to escape from a dying world. They dream of finding a new home where they can begin again.

But over ten thousand light-years from Earth, deep, deep in the heart of space, their starship is confronted by a strange power which threatens their plan.

DREAMTOWN (Fiction Factory 19)

Sheila Gibbs

Hollywood in the early nineteen-fifties. A town full of energy, money, creativity, and thousands of talented young people. Teenager Rosa Valdez lives with her filmstar mother in a luxurious pink marble house with a swimming pool shaped like a giant heart. Life for Rosa is good – too good to last.

One day Rosa's mother finds that she can do no longer get any work. Her name is on a blacklist of so called 'communists' and their 'sympathisers'. Overnight close friends and colleagues turn their backs on Rosa and her mother. Without money Rosa's world collapses around her and she sees what reality is like outside the Hollywood dream.

BLACK LIGHTNING (Fiction Factory 20)

Andrew Monrow

The Skyshoes Sportswear Company is desperate to find a sprinter who has the potential to win the Olympic one hundred meters for them. The winner of this famous race will give Skyshoes global publicity and afterwards greatly increased sales. Skyshoes is at total war with its main rival Adonis Sport for the gigantic world sportswear market. Skyshoes will therefore stop at nothing to win Olympic gold.

An exciting story dealing with commercialism in sport and the problems and dangers of illegal doping.

CHRISTMAS IN HELL (Fiction Factory 6), 1. ed., 5. imp. 1991

Author: Arthur Gordon
Board of editors: Jens Bendtsen, Birte Windfeld-Høeberg (Birte Hasner) and Sig Krug
Educational consultants: Carl Olof Nyman, Henk Werner and Trine Stürup
Linguistic consultant: Laura B. Ricks
Illustrations: Annette Knudsen
Layout: Knud Udbye
Cover design: Sig Krug
Printed in Denmark by Special-Trykkeriet Viborg a-s